PERFORMANCE BOOK

BOOK 5

T0070347

PIANO
Adventures® *by Nancy and Randall Faber*
THE BASIC PIANO METHOD

CONTENTS

FABER
PIANO ADVENTURES®
3042 Creek Drive
Ann Arbor, Michigan 48108

Review Piece

Grace Note Review:

A grace note is an ornamental note that is played quickly into the note that follows.

Review of Form:

Label the **A section** and **B section** before playing the piece.

Allegro!

Allegro in A Major

Johann Wilhelm Hässler
(1747-1822, Germany)
original form

Allegro (♩ = 80-88)

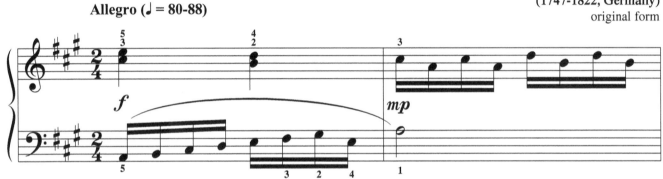

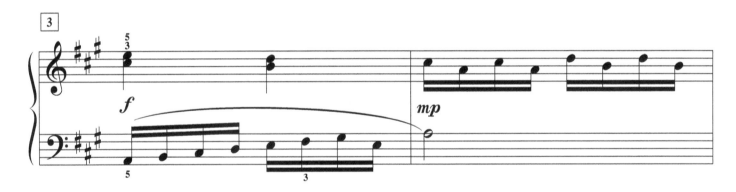

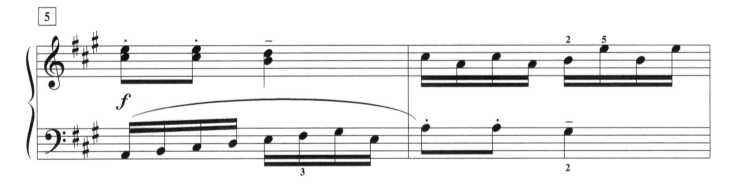

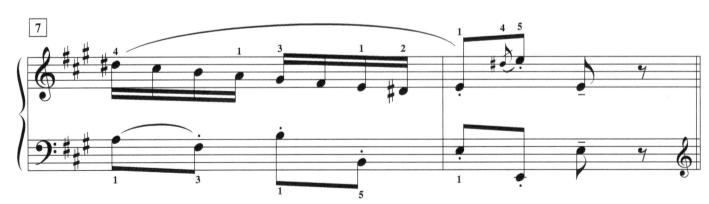

2

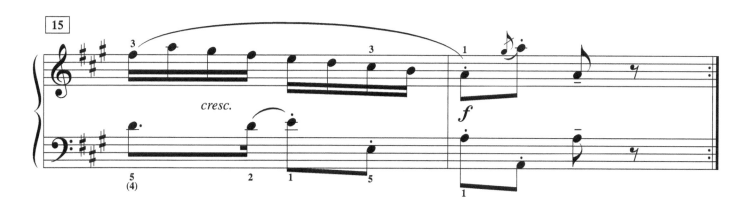

DISCOVERY In this piece, does the **A section** end on the tonic or the dominant? *(circle one)*
Does the **B section** end on the tonic or the dominant? *(circle one)*

Come Back to Sorrento

Ernesto de Curtis
arranged

A minor

Expressively (♩ = 100-112)

cadence on
i* or **V**? *(circle)*

A major

*The small **i** indicates minor.

FF109

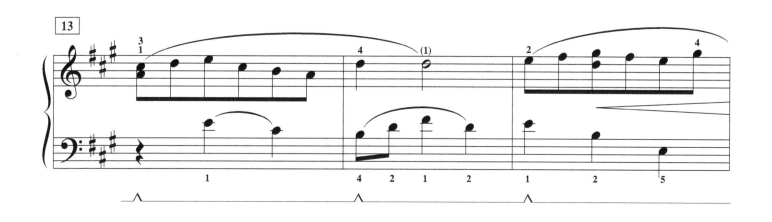

cadence on
I or **V**? *(circle)*

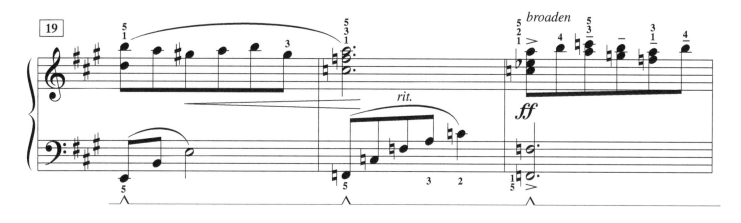

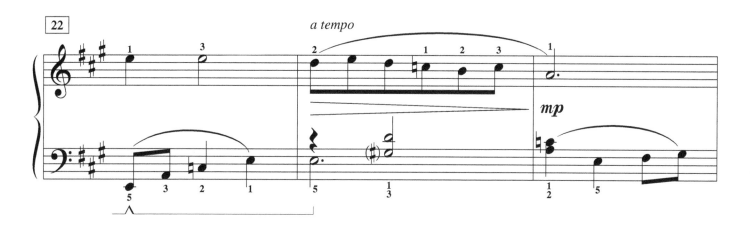

A minor

cadence on
i or **V**? *(circle)*

DISCOVERY

Circle the correct answer for the cadences labeled.

Does the end of the piece cadence on **A major** or **A minor**?

New Tempo Mark:

Lento — very slowly

In a **very slow tempo,** $\frac{12}{8}$ is easier to count as 6 + 6. Feel the "long musical line" of each measure.

Tempo Mark Review

Vivace — very fast

Allegro — fast

Allegretto — cheerful, not as fast as Allegro

Moderato — moderately

Andante — walking speed

Adagio — slowly

Lento — very slowly

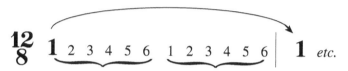

$\frac{12}{8}$ **1** 2 3 4 5 6 1 2 3 4 5 6 | **1** *etc.*

Poetic Theme and Variations

Key of ____ minor

Theme

N. Faber

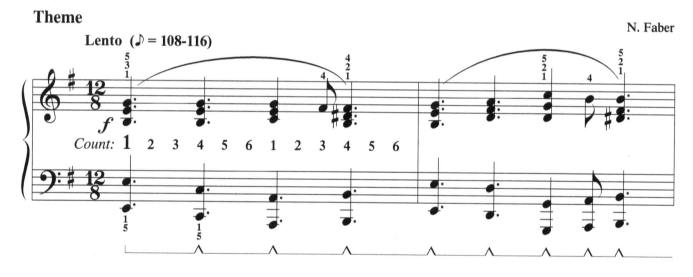

Lento (♪ = 108-116)

Count: 1 2 3 4 5 6 1 2 3 4 5 6

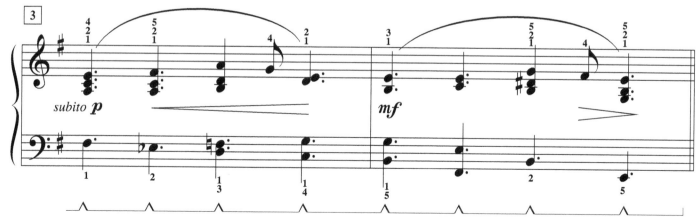

③

subito ***p***   ***mf***

The tenuto marks will help you "voice" (bring out) the melody.

Variation 1 (Lento)

The left hand slurs in this variation show musical patterns.
Do not lift after the slurs, however.
Play the L.H. *legato,* with a long "musical line."

Variation 2 (Lento)

DISCOVERY

Point out a **V - i cadence** in the theme and in each variation.

Appalachian Trail

N. Faber

Find and label an example of each of these intervals:

P4   P5   P8   m3   M6   m7

The harmony of this piece follows the **circle of 5ths**.

The chord names are given for measures 1-8.
Write the root of each chord for measures 9-20.

Reverie* in C

Moderately, with expression ($\quad$ = 80-92)

N. Faber

* In music, a reverie is an instrumental composition of a vague and dreamy character.

FF109?

You've completed the circle of 5ths.

DISCOVERY A *codetta* is a short ending. Where does the *codetta* begin in this piece?

Carnival of the Animals is a set of pieces for two pianos and orchestra. Each piece is named for a different animal. The beautiful melody of *The Swan* is played by the cello.

Performance Hints:

- Play smooth left-hand arpeggios for the harp-like opening.
- Bring out the expressive *cantabile** melody over the soft, murmuring left hand.

The Swan

(from the *Carnival of the Animals*)

Camille Saint-Saëns
(1835-1921, France)
arranged

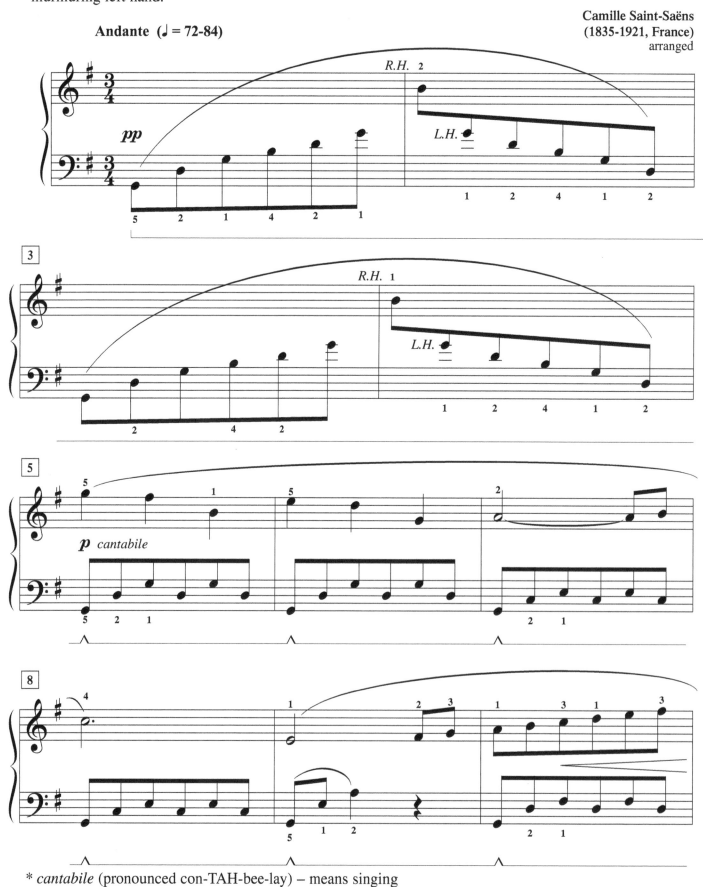

Andante (♩ = 72-84)

* *cantabile* (pronounced con-TAH-bee-lay) – means singing

Lessons p. 28

DISCOVERY

Find and label the following in your music:
a **G major** arpeggio, a **B minor** arpeggio, an **E7** arpeggio.

St. Anthony's Chorale

Franz Joseph Haydn
(1732-1809, Italy)
arranged

maestoso—means majestically

Lessons p. 36

FF1095

cadence on
I or **V**? *(circle)*

cadence on
I or **V**? *(circle)*

DISCOVERY

Put a ✔ above each measure with this rhythm: ♫ ♩ ♫

Muzio Clementi toured widely as a pianist and composer.
While in Vienna, he competed with Mozart and met
Beethoven. In England, he established a piano factory
and a music publishing business.

Waltz in E♭

Muzio Clementi
(1752-1832, Italy)
original form

Lessons p. 40

FF1095

DISCOVERY

Find two descending **E♭ major scales** for the left hand.
Can you play these left-hand passages by memory?

Simple Gifts

Gently moving (♩ = 92-96)

Traditional Shaker Song

Lessons p. 42

FF1095

turn- ing, turn- ing we   come 'round right.

DISCOVERY

Can you play *Simple Gifts* with a friend or family member singing the words?

Boogie Rhythm: The ♫ rhythm is often used in "boogie-woogie" to show *swing*.

♫ = ♩³♪

Bearcat Boogie

Moderate swing (♩ = 132-144)

Faber & Faber

Lessons p. 46

FF1095

DISCOVERY

Measure 29 imitates an earlier measure. Point out that measure.

A *mazurka* is a Polish dance in $\frac{3}{4}$ time. Dotted rhythms and triplets are common in mazurkas.

This mazurka is in the style of Frederic Chopin (SHO-pahn). Chopin is often referred to as the "poet of the piano." He wrote many mazurkas in honor of Poland, his homeland.

Rubato means an expressive "give and take" in the rhythm; a "holding back" and "moving forward" of the tempo.

Hint: First learn the piece with a steady tempo.
　　 Then your teacher will help you add *rubato*.

Mazurka in G Minor

(Homage to Chopin)

Andante expressivo*, with rubato ($\quad$ = 88-96)

N. Faber

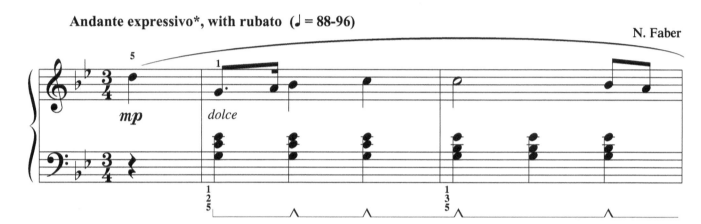

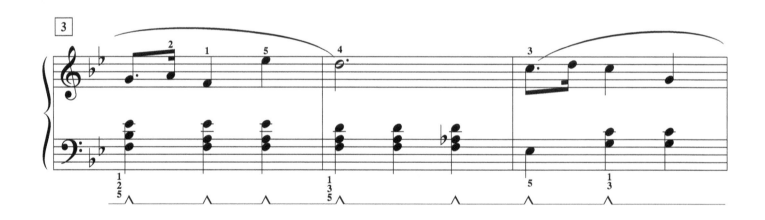

espressivo—means expressively

Cadenza (a showy passage, played freely)

*Ossia indicates an alternate way to play a passage.

For an introduction to Chopin's mazurkas, see:

    Chopin, Three Mazurkas (edited by Randall Faber) from *The Keyboard Artist Library.*

The form of this piece is: **Intro A B A' Coda**

In the A section, the left hand plays the melody while the
right hand accompanies with *blocked chords*. In the return of A,
the right hand accompanies with *arpeggios*. The symbol A'
("A prime") indicates a slightly varied return of A.

Can you label each section in your music?

The Danube Waves

Josif Ivanovici
(1845-1902, Romania)
arranged

Lessons p. 53

FF1095

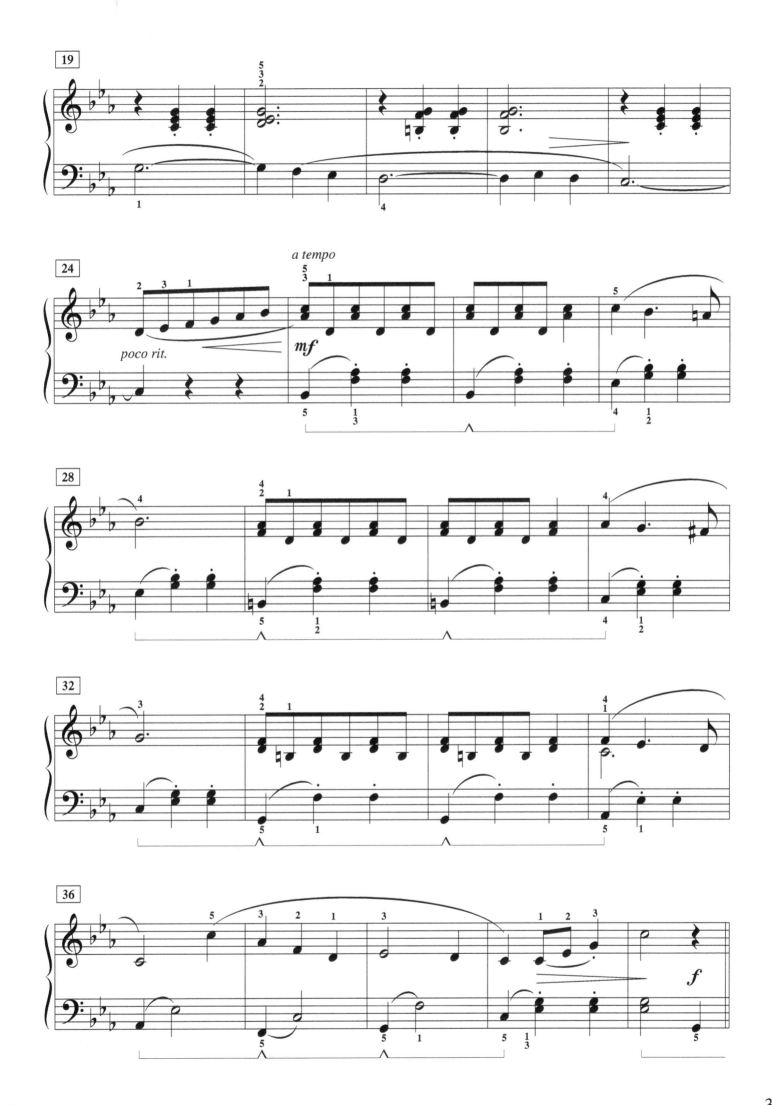

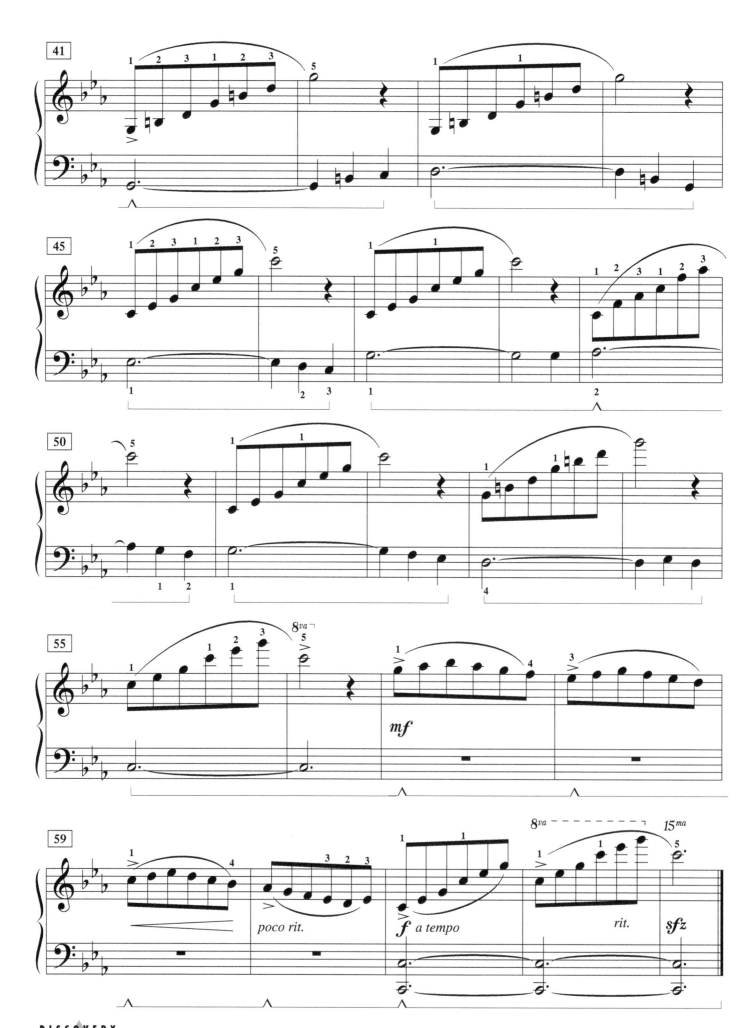

DISCOVERY Write the chord name for each arpeggio on this page.

Hint: Be sure to include a small **m** to indicate a minor harmony.

FF1095